THE CURIOUS
LITTLE BOOK OF WISDOM

THE CUBS FAN'S
LITTLE BOOK OF WISDOM
101 Truths...Learned The Hard Way

by Jim Langford

Diamond Communications, Inc.
South Bend, Indiana
1993

THE CUBS FAN'S LITTLE BOOK OF WISDOM
Copyright © 1993 by Diamond Communications, Inc.

Manufactured in the United States of America
10 9 8 7 6 5 4 3 2

DIAMOND COMMUNICATIONS, INC.
POST OFFICE BOX 88 • SOUTH BEND, INDIANA 46624
(219) 299-9278 • FAX (219) 299-9296

Library of Congress Cataloging-in-Publication Data
Langford, Jim, 1937-
    The Cubs fan's little book of wisdom : 101 truths learned the hard
way / by Jim Langford.
      p.   cm.
    ISBN 0-912083-68-9 : $5.95
    1. Baseball--Quotations, maxims, etc. 2. Chicago Cubs (Baseball
team)--Quotations, maxims, etc. I. Title.
GV867.3.L36 1993
796.357--dc20   93-37864
                                                   CIP

To Trevor Justice and Emily Alice
with a father's love

Yes, I've read and enjoyed H. Jackson Brown's two volumes of *LIFE'S LITTLE INSTRUCTION BOOK*. Though this book is partially patterned after them, it is also quite different. It is one fan's treasury of truths learned from a lifetime wandering with our Chicago Cubs in the desert of the National League. In many cases, I remind readers of an actual event that taught a lesson or inspired an insight worth remembering. In some cases the quote stands by itself; Cubs fans will know why it is included here.

This book is just a beginning. Hundreds of thousands of ardent Cubs fans have no doubt learned other lessons, different truths and additional maxims to live by. I invite you to jot them down and send them to me (P.O. Box 88, South Bend, IN 46624) so that I can collect them in a sequel to this book. Full credit and a free copy will go to everyone whose entry is included.

In the meantime, may this book bring back the joys of seasons past and strengthen the resolve of all who have a big C emblazoned on their heart, to learn and grow and remain true in seasons still to come.

Jim Langford

Don't burden yourself with blame if it isn't your fault.

Unless your name is John Holland, you didn't trade Brock for Broglio.

Humility doesn't require a negative view of self, just an accurate one.

Rogers Hornsby, who hit .380 for the Cubs in 1929, *was* being humble when he said, "Everytime I stepped to the plate, I couldn't help but feel sorry for the pitcher."

3

"It ain't braggin' if you can back it up." ex-Cub Dizzy Dean

No matter how bad the situation is, you can find something positive to say.

General Manager Jim Gallagher said of the 1948 Cubs, "This was the best team ever to finish last in the National League."

The 1993 Mets are living proof that Leo Durocher was wrong:

Bad guys finish last too!

Head for the nearest exit if you hear your company's CEO say something like the following:

"I believe that managers are expendable. In fact, I believe that there should be relief managers so you can keep rotating them." (Cubs owner P.K. Wrigley in 1959, one year before founding the College of Coaches)

As Albert Camus noted,

"There is no fate that cannot be overcome by scorn."

Who really cares about the '69 Mets,
the '84 Padres or the '89 Giants?

Know when to say when.

"When I gave up a grandslam to (Cub) Pete LaCock,
I knew it was time to quit."—Cardinals' great, Bob Gibson

Always behave; you may be somebody's hero.

Recently a friend told me his boyhood idol was Harry Chiti,
a catcher whose weight was higher than his batting average.
As Fred Harris put it, "Chiti looked like everybody's
brother-in-law. And played like him too."

In life as in baseball, good karma doesn't last forever.

The '85 and '90 Cubs are proof enough.

11

Don't expose yourself to ridicule by making idle threats.

On being released by the Cubs, Al Nipper warned, "The Cubs haven't heard the last of me." Actually, they had.

Strength is one thing; controlling it is another.

Roy Smalley, Cubs shortstop of my youth, could throw from the plate to the bleachers on the fly. Unfortunately, he could also throw it to the grandstands from shortstop on the fly. His 51 errors in 1950 remains a record.

Learn the limitations of the "Dance with the one who brought you" theory.

Rick Sutcliffe might have gotten us to the Playoffs in 1984,
but he was exhausted in the sixth inning of Game Five and
Steve Trout was warmed up and ready.
Frey stayed with Sut until it was too late.

Know yourself.

When the Cubs traded pitcher Dave Cole to the
Phillies in 1955, Cole commented sadly, "That's too bad.
They're the only team I can beat." (Two of his three
wins in 1954 were over the Phillies.)

Be grateful for small things.

Imagine if Harry had been doing Cubs games in 1974
when Scipio Spinks came in a trade for Jim Hickman.

16

If you do something really stupid, pretend you did it just to get a laugh.

In 1902 Cubs pitcher Jim St. Vrain decided that since he couldn't hit righthanded, he'd try lefthanded. He actually hit a grounder to short and took off down the baseline. The trouble was, he ran down the line toward third. Shortstop Honus Wagner was stunned: "I'm standing there with the ball in my hand, looking at this guy run from home to third, and for an instant I didn't know where to throw the damn thing." Way to prank 'em, Jimmy!

17

If you have a good hunch, act on it. Don't wait for committee approval.

Asked why the Cubs missed all of the young talent available after World War II, Charlie Grimm explained that the Cubs insisted that a prospect be reviewed by a committee which decided whether or not to sign him. "By that time," Charlie sighed, "Someone else has paid him a bonus and signed him." So while the Cubs pinned their hopes on Smalley, Terwilliger, Mauro and Sawatski, other teams were signing guys like Campanella, Snider, Mays, Ashburn…

Try to generate happiness within yourself.

"If you aren't happy one place, chances are, you won't be happy any place."—Ernie Banks

"Be yourself" is usually good advice—
but not if you're talking to a White Sox, Cardinals or Mets fan.

Do your best to help others do their best.

As Ned Colletti put it, "Check the magic of a winning season and there are always reasons beyond great talent."

Weigh what you say before you say it.

"I think this is going to make us a little more respected."
—Cubs' Bob Kennedy on the Brock-for-Broglio deal

Don't take political correctness to the extreme.

It's O.K. to laugh with Moe Drabowsky when he says,
"I was the second Pole to appear in the World Series.
The first one carried a rake."

23

Don't take even the obvious for granted.

From Bob Ramazzotti, an infielder in the early '50s,
I learned that even popups can be dropped. Often.

Be of good cheer even in a slump.

In 1948 the Cubs offense was so poor that Mgr. Charlie
Grimm sent scouts to comb the minor leagues for help. Soon
he received a wire from a scout: "Spotted a pitcher who stopped a
good team cold. Only one ball was hit out of the infield and
that was a foul fly." Grimm wired back: "Forget the pitcher.
Send the guy who hit the foul."

It's not hard to root for winners;
the test is to be steadfast
when times are bad.

Don't count your chickens...

or as Ernie Banks put it, reflecting on 1969,
"Sometimes you think you have something in
the bag, but the bag breaks."

Don't take a demotion sitting down.

Farmed out to Tacoma in July 1966, pitcher Bill Faul called
his demotion "spiteful and unfair." It came a day after
Bob Skinner had homered off a pitch Faul didn't want to
throw. He shook off the curve, but the catcher called for
the curve again. He threw it and Skinner hit it. He left the
Cubs wondering who it was—the catcher or Durocher—who
had insisted on the ill-fated curve.

28

Have a sense of humor.

Cubs G.M. Wid Matthews in 1952 offered to trade
Bob Rush to Brooklyn for Gil Hodges, Carl Furillo and
Bobby Morgan. (Rebuffed, Wid ended up with a
more modest deal: pitcher Walt Dubiel to the Braves
for pitcher Sheldon Jones.)

You can be a good teammate even to someone you can't stand.

The great keystone combination of Joe Tinker and Johnny Evers went several years without speaking to each other, but they were voted into the Hall of Fame together with Frank Chance.

"Anyone can hit in batting practice."

—Hector Villanueva after several prodigious bp homers

31

Luck is always more abundant
the harder you work.

"Never ridicule a beginner
lest you kill talent
before it develops."
—Knute Rockne

33

You can fail twice in three tries and still lead the league!

Be prepared for your moment in the sun so you can enjoy it.

Though selected for the All-Star team in 1962, George Altman loosened his stirrups as he watched the game from the bench. Called on as a pinch-hitter, he didn't have time to tighten them. Altman hit a home run, but instead of being able to trot around the bases and enjoy it, he had to sprint because his socks were falling down!

Don't let a setback throw you.

In the words of the immortal Bill Caudill, "Even Betty Crocker
burns a cake once in a while."

If you can't beat them or merge with them, acquire them.

In 1956 G.M. Wid Matthews reacquired Russ Meyer who the Cubs had sold in 1949 and who had beaten the Cubs 24 times in 27 decisions. Wid's logic was even if Russ never won a game for the Cubs, at least he wouldn't beat them anymore.

Always leave 'em laughing.

When fired in 1956, Wid Matthews attributed
his fate to seven years of *bad luck*!

38

If you scatter thorns, don't go barefoot.

39

A Cubs fan who can't forgive is a contradiction in terms.

"If you get beat in the first game of
a series, you can't worry about it.
Confidence is everything."

—Mitch Williams

Beware of overconfidence.

Remember how fast a 10 1/2-game lead in August can
become eight games out six weeks later.

Keep your head and stay smooth.

All losing streaks eventually end—and so do winning streaks.

At a certain point in one's career, one can't be the rising star anymore.

Sometimes it's better to be a utility player in Chicago
than a starter in Des Moines.

44

It is better to have swung and missed than never to have swung at all.

Don't boo anyone who is giving 100%.

Did Randy Myers really deserve all those posters?

If you're worried about beating the traffic, stay home and watch it on TV.

Get there for batting practice and stay for the last out!

Don't be fickle.

Real love is steadfast beyond reason.

If you're satisfied with your work performance remember that there's always someone who wants more from you.

Gary Woods led the National League in hitting for a few days in 1984. But one fan in the bleachers wanted more and yelled that if Woods didn't start hitting with more power, the fans would "tear his fx!*ing arm off and put it where the sun doesn't shine!"

Even if you think you'll be out by a mile, hustle.

Sometimes the effort is more important than the result.

Learn tolerance.

As Leo Durocher said of eccentric pitcher Bill Faul in 1966,
"Every team should have some sort of kook on it,
someone who is different, somebody the other guys
can kid about and be relaxed."

Anything can be interesting if you look closely enough.

The big tension on the 1966 Cubs was which Cub hitter
would lead the league in strikeouts. It was so exciting
because it ended in a tie: Adolfo Phillips and
Byron Browne each fanned 133 times.

52

Resist the "misery loves company" temptation.

Don't be glad the Sox lose just on days the Cubs lose too.

Eight heads are not necessarily better than one.

If the College of Coaches taught anything, this is it.

If you rise to the occasion when it counts, people will remember you.

Who will ever forget Willie Smith and his game-winning homer on Opening Day, 1969?

If you're in a job where the people you work with are driving you insane, think about quitting.

Herman Franks said he had enough of Barry Foote, Ted Sizemore and, later, Bill Buckner and so he quit. (Of course, Herman also had a personal fortune in the millions to go home to.)

Don't let tough losses stop you.

Fergie Jenkins lost 1-0 five times in 1968.
But he won 20 games that season anyway.

When you get the prize, don't forget to thank those who helped you along the way.

Remember how Jim Frey and the Cubs circled the field after the last home game in 1984?

Be a realist.

Phil Wrigley reacted to the 1969 Cubs this way: "Naturally I'm disappointed that the Cubs didn't win. By this time, though, I'm used to disappointments."

Keep your eyes open
—especially at home.

In 1950, the Phillies invited a kid from Springfield to work
out for them while they were in Chicago to play the Cubs.
They signed him. He was Robin Roberts.

Be careful what you predict.

Leo Durocher never lived down his famous, "This is not an 8th place ballclub," as his Cubs finished 10th in 1966. A year later, he said only, "We will not win the pennant in 1967."

Stay alert even when you're just warming up.

In 1960 Moe Drabowsky in the bullpen fielded a ball in play, costing teammate Frank Thomas a double.

Accept your role, be a team player and wait for your chance.

Dwight Smith won a starting job with the Cubs;
Jerome Walton spent 1993 at Vancouver.

"Don't alibi on the bad hops; anyone can field the easy ones."

—Mgr. Joe McCarthy

Don't let a bad day rob you of your sense of humor.

Len Merullo once made four errors in one inning, but could still nickname his son, born that day, "Boots."

65

Take your kids to the same
seats at Wrigley where you sat
with your parents.

If you want to boo at Wrigley Field, boo at anyone who brings a portable phone to the game.

67

The optimist always has a better time.

Sing the National Anthem and
"Take Me Out to the Ballgame"
whether or not you have a
good voice.

If you see three balls, swing at the one in the middle.

It worked for Hack Wilson, who hit highballs on the field and off.

Don't wait 'til the last minute to chill the champagne.

Be a believer and have it ready.

71

Never, ever give up.

Think of the dozens of great Cubs comebacks
with two outs in the ninth.

72

Don't rely too heavily on the Law of Averages.

It seems to have been repealed.

Swing for the fences even if you strike out a lot.

As Ralph Kiner said, "Cadillacs are at the end of the bat."

Try to understand the magic of Wrigley Field.

It is sunlight and nightlight, friends,
a few stars and a lot of hope.

75

It's fine to imagine yourself making
a leaping catch at the wall so long
as once in a while you see yourself
as the hitter robbed by that catch.

Tolerate Cardinals fans' right
to love their birdies—at
Busch Stadium.

Even if you lose a heartbreaker, there's always next time.

Cub Bob Hendley pitched a one-hitter against the Dodgers
and lost, 1-0, to a perfect game by Sandy Koufax. But the
next time he faced the Dodgers, Hendley beat 'em, 2-1.
Losing pitcher, Koufax.

Don't let a bad day discourage you.

Billy Williams went 0-for-4 in his first game as a Cub.

"Trying harder when things are going poorly isn't the way to improve performance."

—*The Mental Game of Baseball*

"No high fives until the late innings."

—'Sarge' Matthews

"Stay away from firearms
and don't room higher than
the second floor."

—Frankie Frisch's advice to new managers

82

Managers (and executives): "Never go under .500 if you can help it."

—ex-Mgr. Joe McCarthy

Always keep things in proper perspective.

"You think the Cubs have sore arms? What about the fans in left field?"—Bob Verdi

Beware of frenetic folks.

"Don't mistake activity for achievement."—John Wooden

Aim for the stars.

"In the long run, we hit only what we aim at."—Thoreau.
So let's start using .600 ball as the norm.

Timing is everything.

"You can have money stacked to the ceiling, but the size
of your funeral will still depend on the weather."
—ex-Cub Chuck Tanner

87

When the chips are down, take charge yourself.

Remember Mgr. Gabby Hartnett's homer in the gloamin'?
Or Mgr. Phil Cavarretta's pinch grandslam off Robin Roberts?

Don't be afraid to admit your mistakes.

"If I had known then what I know now, I would never have taken this job."—Mgr. Preston Gomez on resigning with a 38-52 record in 1980

89

When you're tired and it feels like your running on empty, remember Sam Jones.

He hadn't allowed a hit through eight, but opened the ninth
by walking the bases full. He got his no-hitter by
fanning the next three hitters.

Be steadfast but not stubborn.

Remember what happened with six outs to go in the
Playoffs at San Diego. Frey stayed with Sutcliffe while
Trout was ready in the pen.

91

Never play cards with anyone named "Doc," "Ace" or "Branch."

Branch Rickey of the Dodgers and, later, the Pirates outfoxed the Cubs so often that he should have been arrested for interstate fraud. In addition to stealing Andy Pafko, he was able to sell a dozen or more of his minor league castoffs to the Cubs for big money. While Rickey was paying Jackie Robinson $15,000 a year, he was banking $100,000 from the Cubs for Paul Minner and Preston Ward. Later, with the Pirates, Rickey got $100,000 from the Cubs for what was left of Ralph Kiner. For years, the Cubs went back to Rickey again and again, like a moth to fire.

Quit worrying about how much support you get.

In 1917 Cub Hippo Vaughn pitched a no-hitter for nine and lost, 1-0, in the 10th because ex-Cub Fred Toney pitched a no-hitter for 10. A year later, he pitched three complete games in the World Series, gave up a total of three runs and had a record of 1-2.

Go for it even if your dream lasts only a day.

Elder "Bunny" White was the Cubs' Opening Day
shortstop in 1962. He was never heard of before—or since.

Don't blame fate for accidents
unless you're willing to give up
credit for a hole-in-one.

95

People can judge your appearance
and your talents, but no one but
you can know what's really
inside of you.

Demand accountability.

General managers are not elected by the fans who pay
their salaries. Every year there should be a G.M. Day at
Wrigley and the incumbent should circle the field to
accept the verdict of the fans.

97

Stay awake on the job.

Hack Wilson once dozed off in center during a conference on the mound. Unhappy at being yanked, the Cubs pitcher turned and threw the ball off the sign in left center. The startled Wilson, thinking it was in play, raced over and hurried it to second. The crowd loved it. When they love you in Philly, something's wrong!

If you worked hard for it, demand it.

When the Cubs won two and claimed first place in July 1967,
a crowd of 40,000 refused to leave until the Cubs flag was
run up to the top of the Wrigley Field yardarm.
It took an hour, but it got done.

Be suspicious of ballyhoo.

Watch out for Wid Matthews-style euphoria. Sore-armed
Bruce Edwards was going to take the Cubs to the top (he didn't);
"Miksis will fix us" (he didn't); Ellsworth was, "The new Sandy
Koufax" (not quite); Kiner, Gernert and Lennon would wreck
the buildings on Waveland (they stand intact).

Keep at it long enough and you will succeed.

Cub Bob Rush lost 14 straight times to the Phillies before he finally beat them and their ace, Robin Roberts, in 1956.

Don't aggravate people unnecessarily.

Remember, it was Mike Royko's columns about the San Diego
lifestyle that led to the fan frenzy during the 1984
playoffs in Jack Murphy Stadium. Otherwise they'd have
stayed on the beach and the Cubs would've won!